Introduction

BY PETER BUCH

D1563168

Leon Trotsky's views on the Jewish question will be of great interest to radical youth today, especially those of Jewish origin who often feel troubled over the present Arab-Israeli conflict.

The turn toward Marxism within the current international youth radicalization has led many young rebels and Third World liberation fighters to discover the relevance of Trotsky's writings for the revolutionary period we live in now. Trotsky was the first to struggle against Stalin's revision of Marxism and Leninism. He advocated permanent revolution as the road of underdeveloped countries to socialism, and he fought to assemble a new international leadership for the world socialist revolution. Young people who have rallied to the Vietnamese freedom struggle and who cheered Che Guevara's cry for "two, three, . . . many Vietnams" perceive that Trotsky fought, in his day, for "two, three, . . . many" Russian Revolutions. The revolutionary optimism and fighting spirit which emerge from his writings speak directly to today's new generation of fighters.

Trotsky devoted the years of his final exile—from his forcible deportation from the USSR in 1929 till his assassination by an agent of Stalin in 1940—to the struggle to rescue the banner of Leninism from the Stalinist usurpers. The selections in this pamphlet were written during his last ten years, when he was at the height of his powers and engaged in what he regarded as the most significant work of his life, more important even than his role as the organizer of the October 1917 insurrection and the creator of the Red Army.

In his last decade, Trotsky was addressing a generation very different from today's, one which had witnessed the greatest working-class upsurge in history only to see it cruelly smashed, as in Spain, or at least put back in harness, as in the United States.

The European labor movement, captained by either the Stalinized Communist Parties or the reformist social democrats, seemed unable to resist the steady march of capitalist reaction and barbarism which overtook the continent. The entrenchment of the Soviet and Comintern bureaucracies under Stalin had led to the political disarming and physical defeat of the powerful German Communist Party, to the liquidation of Lenin's Old Bolshevik comrades in the Moscow show trials, and finally to the strangulation of promising workers' revolutions in France and Spain which could have flung back the fascist scum.

As the revolutionary tide ebbed and world war approached, millions became deeply disoriented and demoralized. They lost faith in the possibilities of world socialism and the capacity of the working class to take power. In the name of "realism" and "practical politics," old formulas and nostrums long discredited were revived, refurbished, and held up like so many brass icons as the surer promise of survival. In this fantasy world of partition plans, "collective security," disarmament parleys, Munich agreements, "peace in our time," League of Nations "sanctions," and "eternal" peace pacts, Zionism contended for its place too as an alternative to socialist revolution.

And indeed, the regeneration of the most noxious varieties of anti-Semitism by the Nazis victorious in Germany posed the Jewish question anew in the sharpest possible way, as European Jewry faced extinction.

"What should the Jews do now?" many people wondered, overcome by events. "Can they afford to wait for the socialist revolution? What if it doesn't come in time? What if it doesn't come at all? And if it does come, what is to prevent the rise of another tyrant like Stalin, who ordered the repression of entire nationalities, including the Jews? Where can the Jewish refugees go but Palestine, since the doors of all nations are locked to them? Doesn't the threat of Nazi annihilation *prove* the necessity of a Jewish homeland where the Jews can be safe?"

For Trotsky, the Nazi peril, whose enormity he comprehended better and earlier than anyone else, proved more than ever that the Jews would not be safe as long as socialism did not replace capitalism on a world scale. He traced the impending catastrophe to its roots:

"Before exhausting or drowning mankind in blood," he wrote in 1938, "capitalism befouls the world atmosphere with the poisonous vapors of national and race hatred. *Anti-Semitism* today is one of the more malignant convulsions of capitalism's death agony." The strategic task for genuine revolutionaries was clear:

"An uncompromising disclosure of the roots of race prejudice and all forms and shades of national arrogance and chauvinism, particularly anti-Semitism, should become part of the daily work of all sections of the Fourth International, as the most important part of the struggle against imperialism and war. Our basic slogan remains: Workers of the World Unite!" (*The Death Agony of Capitalism and the Tasks of the Fourth International,* adopted by the Founding Conference of the Fourth International, 1938, in *The Transitional Program for Socialist Revolution,* Pathfinder, 1973, 1977.)

But for Trotsky there was no question of "waiting" for socialism. Immediate, practical measures were required to

3

save the Jews from the Nazi butchers. With the defeat of the socialist revolution in Europe, nothing could have helped except a powerful international campaign to spotlight Hitler's actual plans and to force open the doors of the Western countries most able to give asylum, especially the United States and England. Trotsky called for mass action around the demand of asylum *now* for the threatened Jews. Such a demand was capable of uniting all genuine opponents of fascism, socialist or not, in a mass movement which might have saved millions from the gas chambers.

There is no more honorable chapter in the record of world Trotskyism than the energetic campaign to build such a mass movement that it initiated, in united action with many independents, before the war broke out. The campaign was especially active in the U.S., where the racist 1924 immigration laws effectively barred the entry of most Jews.

"Open the gates!" was the slogan carried by the activists of the American Fund for Political Prisoners and Refugees into the union halls, the unemployed councils, the campuses, community groups, and other mass organizations, many of which sent urgent demands to Washington and organized militant demonstrations.

The leaders of the labor, Stalinist, reformist, and Zionist movements for the most part remained aloof from this campaign and thereby condemned it to failure. Their pursuit of "realistic" aims with the methods of "practical politics," i.e., without challenging capitalism, held them strangely immobilized when it came to realizing a concrete "nonsocialist" task around the single issue of rescuing the Jews.

The liberal-labor bloc with Roosevelt was loath to annoy his administration, whose secret war plans might have been hampered by an independent mass movement set in motion by the asylum demand. The Zionists and Jewish community leaders who also lined up with Roosevelt wished neither to embarrass their prospective patron by protesting the racist immigration laws nor to detract from the Jewish colonizing of Palestine by mass Jewish settlement elsewhere. As for the Communist Party, it kept understandably mum about the danger to the Jews from Stalin's new ally after the signing of the Stalin-Hitler pact in 1939. After Hitler's abrogation of that pact in June 1941, the CP leaped onto the Roosevelt bandwagon as his most fervent and loyal booster. Stalin, for his part, tended to soft-pedal the issue as his way of counteracting Hitler's propaganda to the Russians that they were being mobilized to fight only in the interest of the Jews.

Trotsky did not read the Jewish press or follow closely the course of Jewish political affairs. But he was himself of Jewish origin and grew up in the land where the word "pogrom" was coined and anti-Semitism was official. From the beginning, he was involved in the main disputes over the correct road to Jewish emancipation, not least because of the success of the revolutionary cause in winning Jewish adherents in numbers beyond their proportion in the population.

Czarist Russia was known as the "prison house of nations" for its brutal system of national oppression, which singled out the Jews for special persecution as convenient scapegoats for the miseries of the people. Along with many other Jewish youth who joined the revolutionary movement, Trotsky viewed the overthrow of Czarism as the obvious first step to the liberation of the captive peoples, paving the way for the struggle to establish socialism on the entire European continent. Zionism was rejected out of hand because it offered to cooperate with the Czar, instead of overthrowing him, if he would sponsor the Jewish colonization of Palestine.

The most important political organization among the East European Jewish communities at the time was the General Jewish Workers Union of Lithuania, Poland, and Russia, known as the Bund. It demanded full rights for the Jews where they lived and worked, and it fiercely opposed Zionism as a utopian, reactionary scheme, a form of self-expulsion, preached by Jewish bourgeois nationalists who played into the hands of the anti-Semites and further divided the working class.

Until the rise of Hitler and the coming of the Second World War, Zionism remained a definite minority trend among the Jewish people, especially the Jewish workers, who were violently opposed to it. During the war, the Bund disappeared in the fires that consumed East European Jewry, but in prerevolutionary Russia it played a key role among the Jewish workers. To clarify some of Trotsky's remarks, and much of Lenin's writings, on the Jewish question, it is worthwhile to dwell briefly on their dispute with the Bund.

In the historic Second Congress of the Russian Social Democrats in 1903, where the division into Bolsheviks (Majority) and Mensheviks (Minority) occurred, the Bund opposed Lenin's concept of a multinational, democratically centralized, professional revolutionary party. The Bundists favored a federated party structure and insisted on taking exclusive charge of party relations with the Jewish working class. It advocated "national-cultural autonomy" to unite the Jews scattered throughout the whole country, not in a territory of their own, but around schools and other institutions, a concept later championed by the Austrian social democratic theoretician, Otto Bauer. Ironically, the reformist Bauer opposed the right of national self-determination, the essence of which was the right of secession, and proposed his scheme instead as a substitute more acceptable to the liberal bourgeoisie who were anxious to keep the Austro-Hungarian Empire intact.

Trotsky, then still in his twenties, sided with Lenin in this dispute and, in fact, was the majority spokesman at the Congress against the Bund, which later walked out and lined up with the Mensheviks.

In a subsequent article directed against the Bund, "The Decomposition of Zionism and Its Possible Successors," in *Iskra,* January 1904, Trotsky quoted a current Bund pamphlet on the Sixth Zionist Congress in Basle. The Bund authors declared that the "liquidation" of Zionism had begun, but that the "real interests hidden under the name of Zionism" would remain and find successors. Trotsky agreed that "Zionism has exhausted its impoverished content and the Basle Congress . . . was a demonstration of its decomposition and its impotence." But he went on to point out that the Bund's demand to act as the sole representative of the Jewish workers to the party instead of the party's organizational representative to the Jewish workers, as had been its original function, was a concession to the bourgeois nationalist spirit of Zionism, despite the Bund's fierce anti-Zionism. Its policies would prove unable to win over and educate the disappointed left Zionist currents then coming over to the revolutionary ranks. The Bund itself, he warned, could well become that feared successor to Zionism which would act to "divert the Jewish proletariat from the path of revolutionary Social Democracy. . . ."

Trotsky was wrong, of course, along with the Bund and the Bolsheviks, in regarding Zionism as a dead cause. The unforeseen delay in the advent of world socialism was to give it a new lease on life—at a staggering cost to the Jewish people. But Trotsky was right about the Bund. In 1917 it formed a bloc with the Mensheviks against the socialist October Revolution, placing unwarranted confidence in the ability of the national democratic regime set up in February to grant the equal rights and liberation of nationalities it had promised.

"For the oppressed nations of Russia," Trotsky wrote in 1932, "the overthrow of the monarchy inevitably meant also their own national revolution. In this matter, however, we observe the same thing as in all other departments of the February regime: the official democracy, held in leash by its political dependence upon an imperialist bourgeoisie, was totally incapable of breaking the old fetters. Holding inviolable its right to settle the fate of all other nations, it continued jealously to guard those sources of wealth, power and influence which had given the Great Russian bourgeoisie its dominant position . . ."

This regime, headed by Kerensky, did seek to annul the repressive laws and establish formal juridical equality among the peoples before the state. "This formal equality gave most of all to the Jews," Trotsky said, "for the laws limiting their rights had reached the number of 650. Moreover, being city dwellers and the most scattered of all the nationalities, the Jews could make no claim either to state independence or even territorial autonomy. As to the project of a so-called 'national-cultural autonomy,' . . . this reactionary utopia . . . melted in those first days of freedom like wax under the sun's rays.

"But a revolution is a revolution for the very reason that it is not satisfied either with doles or deferred payments. The abolition of the more shameful national limitations established a formal equality of citizens regardless of their nationality, but this revealed only the more sharply the unequal position of the nationalities as such, leaving the major part of them in the position of step-children or foster-children of the Great Russian state." (*The History of the Russian Revolution*, Pathfinder, 1980, pp. 1035–36.)

To establish the social basis for the genuine equality of nations as well as to defend the gains already achieved, the national democratic revolution had to break with capitalism and "grow over," as Trotsky put it in explaining this process of *permanent* revolution, into a socialist revolution. The Bolsheviks were the only party prepared to take the leadership of such a revolution and to defend it in the civil war that followed when the old ruling classes launched a violent campaign to overthrow the new workers' government.

The most advanced sections of the oppressed nationalities, including the Jews, came forward to support and defend this next phase of the struggle, often in the form of their own military battalions. Trotsky explained his approach to these formations in a telegram he sent as head of the Red Army on May 10, 1919, to the Military Headquarters in Kiev:

"Since the Jewish S.R. [Socialist Revolutionary] party, 'Poale Zion,' and other Jewish workers' organizations announced their readiness to organize sections of the Jewish workers to defend the revolution, I propose to organize such formations under the authority of the (military) Headquarters. Along with this proposal, I suggest that the Jewish battalions enter those regiments where there are also battalions of other nationalities. In this way we can avoid the chauvinism which results from the estrangement of the different nationalities, and which unfortunately arises when entirely independent national military units are formed." (Quoted in *The Pogroms in the Ukraine in the Year 1919,* by Elias Tcherikower, YIVO Press, 1965.)

Trotsky never swerved from his conviction that the struggle for Jewish emancipation was inseparably linked with the fate of the struggle for socialism. The attitude of Lenin and the Bolsheviks toward the national question flowed from the same kind of perspective, which Trotsky contrasted, in one of his last works, to the liberal position of the Austrian reformists:

"One of the aims of the Austrian program of 'cultural autonomy' was 'the preservation and development of the national idiosyncrasies of peoples.' Why and for what purpose? asked Bolshevism in amazement. Segregating the various nationalistic portions of mankind was never our concern. True, Bolshevism insisted that each nation should have the right to secede—the right, but not the duty—as the ultimate, most effective guarantee against oppression. But the thought of artificially preserving national idiosyncrasies was profoundly alien to Bolshevism. The removal of any, even disguised, even the most refined and practically 'imponderable' national oppression or indignity, must be used for the revolutionary unification rather than the segregation of the workers of various nationalities. Wherever national privileges and injuries exist, nations must have the possibility to separate from each other, that thus they may facilitate the free unification of the workers, in the name of a close rapprochement of nations, with the distant perspective of the eventual complete fusion of all. Such was the basic tendency of Bolshevism, which revealed the full measure of its force in the October revolution." (*Stalin*, 1940.)

The right of nations to self-determination was not proclaimed by Lenin's party, however, in the manner of a benign guarantee to be accepted gratefully and at face value by dependent peoples. Trotsky emphasized that in these words:

"What characterizes Bolshevism on the national question is that in its attitude towards the oppressed nations, even the most backward, it considers them not only the object but also the subject of politics. Bolshevism does not confine itself to recognizing their 'right' to self-determination and to parliamentary protests against the trampling upon of this right. Bolshevism penetrates into the midst of the oppressed nations; it raises them up against their oppressors; it ties up their struggle with the struggle of the proletariat in capitalist countries; it instructs the oppressed Chinese, Hindus, or Arabs in the art of insurrection and it assumes full responsibility for this work in the face of civilized executioners. Here only does Bolshevism begin, that is, revolutionary Marxism in action." ("What Next? Vital Questions for the German Proletariat," in *The Struggle Against Fascism in Germany*, Pathfinder, 1971.)

Unfortunately, the Russian Revolution was not followed by victorious socialist revolutions in other countries which could have helped the first workers' state to overcome its inherited backwardness, its postwar devastation, and the capitalist embargo that isolated it from the world market. Nurtured by these conditions, a privileged nationalist-minded bureaucracy headed by Stalin usurped party leadership and took over governmental power. Although they spouted Leninist rhetoric, the new Stalinist leaders no longer instructed the oppressed in the art of insurrection, but rather commanded their sacrifices to win short-lived diplomatic concessions from the imperialist powers, all in pursuit of the preposterous notion that "socialism in one country" could be built peacefully in an imperialist world environment. The Communist Third International, or Comintern, founded by Lenin in 1919 as a world party for socialist revolution, was gradually reduced to a Moscow-controlled pressure agency to serve the immediate diplomatic needs of the Stalin regime.

In the Soviet Union, the Communist Left Opposition, headed by Trotsky, was crushed after a long inner-party struggle. Trotsky was then forcibly exiled to Turkey, where he immediately directed his appeal to Communists abroad. Among those to respond were groups of Yiddish-speaking

Communist workers in France and the United States.

The first selections in this pamphlet are letters to the Yiddish-language newspapers put out by these groups, *Klorkeit* (Clarity) in Paris and *Unser Kamf* (Our Struggle) in New York. Trotsky wrote these at a time when he still hoped to rally forces within the Comintern to reverse the Stalinist trend and take advantage of the new revolutionary opportunities opening up with the world capitalist crisis of the 1930s. The Trotskyists still functioned as a left opposition within the Communist parties, directing their appeals to the Communist ranks against their unjust expulsion and for a return to the genuine principles of Bolshevism. In the United States at that time they were organized into the Communist League of America, whose English-language organ was *The Militant,* which directed its message to the Jewish workers through *Unser Kamf.*

The left Zionists advocated emigration to Palestine because, in their view, the Jewish workers and radicals in Western society could not be effective in the class struggles in their own countries, where they were regarded as aliens. These letters show that Trotsky, on the contrary, saw in the "pariah status" of the Jewish and other minority workers a special revolutionary force where proper leadership could play a decisive role in the battle for socialism.

All the remaining selections in this collection date from after 1933, when the ignominious capitulation of the German CP to Hitler without a fight led Trotsky to conclude that there was no hope left for salvaging the Comintern and to call instead for the founding of a new, Fourth International.

"On the 'Jewish Problem'" is an interview done in France in 1934 and one of Trotsky's earliest statements dealing with the Arab-Jewish conflict in Palestine as well as with the new argument that the rise of German fascism compelled a revision of the traditional Marxist opposition to Zionism.

Later in 1934 ("Reply to a Question About Birobidjan"), Trotsky answered an inquiry about the correct attitude to take toward the project of a separate territory in Birobidjan for settling Jews who wished to live together and develop their culture as an ethnic community.

Upon Trotsky's arrival in Mexico in January 1937, a group of Jewish journalists submitted a series of questions to Trotsky about his attitude to Jewish assimilation and nationhood, anti-Semitism in the Soviet Union, and Birobidjan. In the "Interview with Jewish Correspondents in Mexico," Trotsky admitted that he had changed his original expectation of a "quasi-automatic" disappearance of the Jewish question by the process of assimilation. He granted that through the development of Yiddish-speaking culture a Jewish nation had in fact been formed, though it lacked a territorial base. Some people have misinterpreted this as a change in Trotsky's opposition to Zionism, but the interview speaks for itself on that score.

In "Thermidor and Anti-Semitism," written in 1937, Trotsky combatted the thinly veiled anti-Semitism of the Stalin faction, to which its liberal admirers abroad were blind and to which opponents of Marxism eagerly pointed as evidence that socialism was no answer for the Jewish problem.

"Thermidor" was the month, according to the new calendar proclaimed by the French bourgeois revolution, in which the radical Jacobins led by Robespierre were overthrown by a reactionary wing within the revolution that did not go so far, however, as to restore the feudal regime. Trotsky used the term as a historical analogy, to designate the seizure of power by the conservative Stalinist bureaucracy within the framework of nationalized property relations. Since capitalist property relations were not restored,

Trotsky advocated *unconditional* defense of the workers' states against the imperialist governments, while he called at the same time for a *political* revolution to throw out the Stalin bureaucracy, whose ruinous policies strengthened the danger of capitalist restoration.

In December, 1938, a few months after the founding of the Fourth International, Trotsky directed an urgent "Appeal to American Jews Menaced by Fascism and Anti-Semitism." He warned that the Jews faced physical extermination not only in Europe but also in the United States. Anti-Semitic demagogues in America like Father Coughlin already had a mass following and stood ready to summon their fascist gangs into action against the Jews as well as labor at the next major downturn in the extended economic crisis gripping the country.

Trotsky asked for support, especially financial support, for the new international, which had not stopped at asserting the need for socialism as the salvation of the Jews but had proceeded to formulate a transitional program which could be implemented immediately.

The fate of the Jews is linked to the fate of the working class, Trotsky declared. Help the revolutionary vanguard to promote the self-confidence, activity, and audacity of the oppressed, to mobilize the workers' physical resistance to the fascists, to turn back the wave of reaction that menaced world Jewry! The broad campaign, discussed above, for granting immediate asylum to the Jewish refugees, especially the German Jews who stood in imminent peril, had already been launched by sections of the Fourth International.

The Second World War descended with all its horror on Europe as the decade of the thirties closed. In May 1940, the Emergency Conference of the Fourth International convened despite great hardships to assess the new turn of events and orient the revolutionary vanguard. The conference prepared a manifesto to the world working class, drafted by Trotsky, on the nature of the imperialist war and the factors that could lead to its transformation into a struggle for the world socialist revolution. At the same time, the manifesto called for action along the lines of strategic and tactical directives worked out at the conference. Key sections of the manifesto analyzed the source and role of anti-Semitism; these are excerpted here in "Imperialism and Anti-Semitism."

A month before his death in August 1940, Trotsky assessed once more the chances of Jewish salvation in Palestine. In a fragment found among his papers afterwards, he wrote:

"The attempt to solve the Jewish question through the migration of Jews to Palestine can now be seen for what it is, a tragic mockery of the Jewish people. Interested in winning the sympathy of the Arabs who are more numerous than the Jews, the British government has sharply altered its policy toward the Jews, and has actually renounced its promise to help them found their 'own home' in a foreign land. The future development of military events may well transform Palestine into a bloody trap for several hundred thousand Jews. Never was it so clear as it is today that the salvation of the Jewish people is bound up inseparably with the overthrow of the capitalist system." (July 1940.)

As it turned out, only the fortuitous shift of forces in the war ultimately halted the German army's advance toward the conquest of the Middle East and exempted Palestine itself from becoming a devastated battleground. The Zionist program, however, proved to be of little aid in saving six million Jews from the "bloody trap" in Europe and did much to obscure the genuine solution to the Jewish problem. The Zionists helped to shift attention away from the real cause of

Jewish persecution, namely, the malignant contradictions of capitalism, and asserted that it was instead the national homelessness of the Jews, i.e., a mere national "defect" of the Jews themselves, which generated the feverish passions directed against them.

The relationship of forces in the Middle East has changed since Trotsky wrote. Israel is a strong, apparently invincible power. Her people, once among the chief victims of the imperialist doctrine of "lebensraum," have now ironically been maneuvered once again into the position of middle-men—the old stereotype from which Zionism promised to deliver them—in transmitting this hateful racist doctrine to the Arab Palestinians. These are the homeless people now, expelled to make way for the Jewish settlers. Israel functions as the most stable and dependable ally—for the present—of American interests in the Middle East. At bottom, however, it is a small, dependent nation that has lent itself as an instrument against the Arab revolution. Hated by the millions of Arab workers, peasants, and students both inside and outside its borders, Israel can be flung aside at the next juncture when and if U.S. imperialism deems it expendable. Israel remains . . . a "bloody trap."

The original Zionist vision of creating a unique new Jewish identity freely determined by Jews reunited with the land and engaged in productive labor cannot be fulfilled in a garrison state, dependent upon American imperialism, driven by Zionist exclusionism and chauvinism, and internally regimented for the needs of an aggressive capitalist nation-state.

On the other hand, the establishment of Israel has not made the Jews abroad any safer. In the capitalist countries, a severe social crisis could produce the same conditions of widespread unemployment, middle-class ruin, and national desperation which spurred the Hitlerite reaction and anti-Semitic frenzy in Germany. A profit-motivated society which concentrates the national wealth and means of production in the hands of a few rival capitalist oligarchies cannot avoid such crises and will continue to breed war, depression, racism, and finally anti-Semitism.

As for the Soviet bloc, the ruling bureaucracy there is not above the use of thinly disguised anti-Semitism to reinforce its domination and stifle dissent.

"The salvation of the Jewish people cannot come from reliance upon Zionist chauvinism, American imperialism, or Stalinist bureaucratism. Every expedient short of the struggle for socialism, any substitute for that, will end in calamity for the Jews." So writes the noted American Marxist George Novack in a recent essay, *How Can the Jews Survive? A Socialist Answer to Zionism* (Pathfinder, 1969).

"The Jews have to link themselves," Novack concludes, "with those forces in their own country and on a world scale that are fighting to overthrow imperialism and striving to build the new society. The solution of the Jewish question is indissolubly bound up with the complete emancipation of humanity that can be brought about only along the road of international socialism."

The present generation of revolutionary youth, both Jewish and non-Jewish, have already given much evidence that they are determined to follow that road.

April 1970

Letter to 'Klorkeit' and to the Jewish workers in France

This letter of May 10, 1930, appeared in Klorkeit, *no. 3, Paris, May 1930, under the heading "The Role of the Jewish Workers Within the General Workers' Movement in France."*

Dear Comrades:

Many thanks for your thorough and interesting letter which for the first time gave me a review of the Jewish workers' movement in Western Europe. I rejoice at the tone of active optimism which emerges from the lines and which certainly reflects the spirit of your organization. In addition, Comrade Fr. [Pierre Frank] has already related to me with great sympathy the militant spirit of the Jewish Opposition Group in Paris.

The idea of transforming *Klorkeit* into an international Jewish organ is an interesting one. But as yet I have no clear view of the relationship this would have to the national movements and to the Opposition organizations involved. The more *Klorkeit* becomes "international" in the technical sense, the more it will have to assume a theoretic-propagandistic character, because it will naturally not be able to deal with the specific political questions of each separate country.

I maintain that it is without a doubt the greatest obligation of the Jewish workers in France, just as in other countries, to participate in the workers' movement of the land in which they live, work and struggle. Do the Jewish workers in France, in their majority, consider themselves permanent immigrants, or do they expect to leave the country in the near future? I believe the first is more correct. If this is the case, it is very important to acquire the French language. In the given situation, this is not only in the individual interest of each person, but also in the political interest of the French and international working class. Sixty thousand Jewish workers in Paris is a great force. The foreign workers in France will represent above all a very great factor in the development of the country, even more powerful than the Negroes in America, with whom they have in common only their pariah status.

Traditionally the purely French organizations do not have a mass character. To an extent they are based on a political and trade union "aristocracy" of the working class. The overwhelming majority remain unorganized and distant from the activities of the political and trade union organizations. In France this is the cardinal question. It seems to me that the role the foreign workers play in France today will shake up the country's strong conservatism. Since the foreign workers represent in their greatest majority the lower layers of the country's proletariat, they are thereby close to, tied to, and share the same fate as the bottom layers of the native proletariat, which remains, however, most distant from the official organizations. The foreign workers are of a different mind, just because they are foreign; of an emigrant spirit, more mobile, more receptive to revolutionary ideas. That is why the ideology of communism can gain the respect of the foreign workers and can make them a powerful instrument in penetrating the whole French working class.

Your group as well as the other groups must have a clear appreciation of this great historic mission. Naturally, not in the spirit of some national messianic pride—there can be no talk of that—but in the spirit of a great international obligation. In this connection I posed the question of the character of *Klorkeit*. It will of course not serve to tear away the Jewish workers from the workers' movement of the specific countries, as was previously the case with the press of the Jewish "Bund," but on the contrary—to bring them into the life of that working class.

As regards the general Opposition, it must find among the foreign workers a field of work that is not only important but also very opportune. The bureaucratism of the official party [Communist Party—Ed.] organization, which devastates everything, must first of all hit hardest at the weakest part, and these are naturally the foreign workers. Since the latter are, because of their socially inferior position, more inclined to be critical, I believe that it is possible through a great, conscious, and truly self-sacrificing action to build up the Opposition as the crystallized center of the majority of the foreign workers.

My heartfelt greetings to all the members of the group. Yours,

L. Trotsky
(Prinkipo, Turkey)

Greetings to 'Unser Kamf'

Trotsky's salute to Unser Kamf, *the Yiddish-language Opposition paper published in New York, was written May 9, 1932, and the translation below was published in* The Militant *on June 11, 1932.*

Dear Comrades:

The appearance of your paper was of itself a very important step forward. The first successes of the paper show that it was a necessity. Yes, and could it have been doubted even for a minute?

The Jewish workers in the United States are a large and important part of the whole proletariat of the country. Historical conditions have made the Jewish workers susceptible to the ideas of scientific Communism. The very fact of the dispersement of the Jewish workers in a number of countries should instill in them and does instill in them the ideas of *internationalism.* In view of just this alone the Communist Left Opposition has every reason to count on a big influence among the Jewish proletarians in the United States. What characterizes the Left Opposition primarily is its profound international character. Precisely because of this it must speak in every national language. The existence of an independent Jewish publication serves not to separate the Jewish workers, but on the contrary to make available to them those ideas which combine all the workers in one international revolutionary family. You, it is understood, reject decisively and intransigently the old Bundist principle of federation of the national organization. The Jewish workers won over by your paper must struggle in the general ranks of the Communist League and the mass organizations of the American proletariat. Insofar as your paper will develop and strengthen, it may also assume significance beyond the boundaries of the United States and Canada: in South America, in Europe and Palestine. In the economic sense and in the sense of civil rights, the Jewish workers are a weak link of the proletariat. The policy of the bureaucratized Comintern reflects itself most disastrously on the most oppressed and disfranchised part of the proletariat: in Poland, in the Baltic regions, in France, evidently also in Palestine. The working class cannot march towards its liberation by command. Revolutionary courage and political will can be strengthened only with the aid of creative ideas which the workers must learn independently through criticism, deliberation and examination by experience. Without this, the very sources of the movement inevitably dry up. And we see in actuality how the largest national sections of the Comintern, in spite of the exceptionally favorable circumstances, suffer defeat after defeat.

The workers are capable of withstanding the harshest political blows if they have the possibility of thinking through the reasons for failure and independently extracting from it all the necessary conclusions for the future. But the curse lies in the fact that the bureaucracy of the Comintern is not only incapable of leading the workers to victory, but cannot even permit them to think through the reasons for defeat. After each new blow of the enemies, the Centrist [Stalinist] bureaucracy on its part hits the workers over the skull, prohibiting them from thinking, criticizing and learning. This criminal regime becomes the chief source of disappointment and apathy. The first victims of the blows from the class enemy as well as from the Centrist bureaucracy, as already said, are the weakest links of the working class.

Your paper is the organ of the Communist League. Its immediate task is to gather the Jewish workers in America under the banner of Marx and Lenin. The more successfully this work is carried out the sooner it will rise to an international height, the more the ideas of the Left Opposition will penetrate into the midst of the Jewish workers of the Old World, the USSR included.

With my whole heart I greet your paper and I shall try to be useful in your work with everything I can. Yours,

L. Trotsky
(Prinkipo, Turkey)

On the 'Jewish problem'

This interview appeared in Class Struggle, *February 1934. The journal was the organ of a short-lived group, the Communist League of Struggle, led by Albert Weisbord.*

QUESTION: Does the Left Opposition have to make special demands to win the Jewish working class in America?

ANSWER: The role of the foreign-born Jewish worker in the American proletarian revolution will be a very great one, and in some respects decisive. There is no question but that the Left Opposition must do all it can to penetrate into the life of the Jewish workers.

QUESTION: What is your attitude towards the Jewish language? Why do you in your autobiography characterize it as "jargon"?

ANSWER: My attitude towards the Jewish language is similar to that of all languages. If I really used in my autobiography the term "jargon," it is because in the years of my youth in Odessa the Jewish language was not called Yiddish, as today, but "jargon." Such was the expression of Jews themselves, who did not consider it a sign of superciliousness. The word Yiddish is in universal use for the last fifteen or twenty years. I can see this even in France.

QUESTION: In the Jewish circles you are considered to be an "assimilator." What is your attitude towards assimilation?

ANSWER: I do not understand why I should be considered as an "assimilator." I do not know, generally, what kind of a meaning this word holds. I am, it is understood, opposed to Zionism and all such forms of self-isolation on the part of the Jewish workers. I call upon the Jewish workers of France to better acquaint themselves with the problems of French life and of the French working class. Without that it is difficult to participate in the working class movement of that country in which they are being exploited. As the Jewish proletariat is spread in different countries it is necessary for the Jewish worker, outside of his own language, to strive to know the language of other countries as a weapon in the class struggle. What has that to do with "assimilation"?

QUESTION: The official Communist Party characterized, without question, the Jewish-Arab events in 1929 in Palestine as the revolutionary uprising of the oppressed Arabian masses. What is your opinion of this policy?

ANSWER: Unfortunately, I am not thoroughly familiar with the facts to venture a definite opinion. I am now studying the question. Then it will be easier to see in what proportion and in what degree there were present those elements such as national liberationists (anti-imperialists) and reactionary Mohammedans and anti-Semitic pogromists. On the surface, it seems to me that all these elements were there.

QUESTION: What is your attitude about Palestine as a possible Jewish "homeland" and about a land for the Jews generally? Don't you believe that the anti-Semitism of German fascism compels a different approach to the Jewish question on the part of Communists?

ANSWER: Both the fascist state in Germany, as well as the Arabian-Jewish struggle, bring forth new and very clear verifications of the principle that the Jewish question cannot be solved within the framework of capitalism. I do not know whether Jewry will be built up again as a nation. However, there can be no doubt that the material conditions for the existence of Jewry as an independent nation could be brought about only by the proletarian revolution. There is no such thing on our planet as the idea that one has more claim to land than another.

The establishment of a territorial base for Jewry in Palestine or any other country is conceivable only with the migrations of large human masses. Only a triumphant socialism can take upon itself such tasks. It can be foreseen that it may take place either on the basis of a mutual understanding, or with the aid of a kind of international proletarian tribunal which should take up this question and solve it.

The blind alley in which German Jewry finds itself as well as the blind alley in which Zionism finds itself is inseparably bound up with the blind alley of world capitalism, as a whole. Only when the Jewish workers clearly see this interrelationship will they be forewarned against pessimism and despair.

Reply to a question about Birobidjan

The translations of the replies below were found among the papers of the late John G. Wright. The inquiry was sent to the Paris editorial office of the Bulletin of the Opposition, *organ of the Russian Bolshevik Leninists, by a group of Jewish Left Oppositionists, who signed themselves "Ykslagor," working within the Soviet Union under conditions of severe repression. Trotsky's reply was written in October 1934. The reply by "Schwartz" (pen name of Leon Sedov, Trotsky's son) refers to the "Gezerd," which was the Yiddish name for the OZET, or "Association for the Rural Placement of Jewish Toilers," set up in 1926 to handle Jewish settlement in Birobidjan and dissolved by Stalin in 1938–39 as a "hotbed" of Trotskyist and other opposition elements.*

Letter by Leon Trotsky

With respect to the letter by Ykslagor: the statement that Birobidjan is "Left Zionism" seems to me to be completely incorrect. Zionism draws away the workers from the class struggle by means of unrealizable hopes of a Jewish state under capitalist conditions. But a workers' government is duty bound to create for the Jews, as for any nation, the very best circumstances for cultural development. This means, inter alia: to provide for those Jews who desire to have their own schools, their own press, their own theatre, etc., a separate territory for self-administration and development. The international proletariat will behave in the same way when it will become the master of the whole globe. In the sphere of the national question there must be no restraint; on the contrary there must be an all-sided material assistance for the cultural needs of all nationalities and ethnic groups. If this or that national group is doomed to go down (in the national sense) then this must proceed in the same way as a natural process, but never as a consequence of any territorial, economic, or administrative difficulties.

L. Trotsky

Editorial Office
Opposition Bulletin of the Bolshevik Leninists
Ykslagor:

Dear Comrades,
Your letter was duly received and if we did not answer you immediately, this was due only to the fact that we are working under exceptionally difficult conditions. In connection with your question about Birobidjan we wanted to give you an authoritative reply. The author of this reply, as you know, lives and works under the most difficult conditions. This is the explanation for the lateness of our reply to you. With regard to your other question of rejoining the Gezerd—we are not in a position to give our opinion, due to scanty information. We shall try our best to reply on this question as soon as we receive the necessary information. . . .

With comradely greetings,
Schwartz

Interview with Jewish correspondents in Mexico

This interview, done January 18, 1937, is printed below as it appeared in the magazine Fourth International, *December 1945. The correspondents represented the ITA (Jewish Telegraphic Agency) and* Der Weg, *a Jewish paper published in Mexico. A Yiddish version of the interview also appeared in the Jewish liberal daily* Der Tog, *and in the socialist daily* Forwaerts, *January 24, 1937.*

Before trying to answer your questions I ought to warn you that unfortunately I have not had the opportunity to learn the Jewish language, which moreover has been developed only since I became an adult. I have not had and I do not have the possibility of following the Jewish press, which prevents me from giving a precise opinion on the different aspects of so important and tragic a problem. I cannot therefore claim any special authority in replying to your questions. Nevertheless I am going to try and say what I think about it.

During my youth I rather leaned toward the prognosis that the Jews of different countries would be assimilated and that the Jewish question would thus disappear in a quasi-automatic fashion. The historical development of the last quarter of a century has not confirmed this perspective. Decaying capitalism has everywhere swung over to an exacerbated nationalism, one part of which is anti-Semitism. The Jewish question has loomed largest in the most highly developed capitalist country of Europe, in Germany.

On the other hand the Jews of different countries have created their press and developed the Yiddish language as an instrument adapted to modern culture. One must therefore reckon with the fact that the Jewish nation will maintain itself for an entire epoch to come. Now the nation cannot normally exist without a common territory. Zionism springs from this very idea. But the facts of every passing day demonstrate to us that Zionism is incapable of resolving the Jewish question. The conflict between the Jews and Arabs in Palestine acquires a more and more tragic and more and more menacing character. I do not at all believe that the Jewish question can be resolved within the framework of rotting capitalism and under the control of British imperialism.

And how, you ask me, can socialism solve this question? On this point I can but offer hypotheses. Once socialism has become master of our planet or at least of its most important sections, it will have unimaginable resources in all domains. Human history has witnessed the epoch of great migrations on the basis of barbarism. Socialism will open the possibility of great migrations on the basis of the most developed technique and culture. It goes without saying that what is here involved is not compulsory displacements, that is, the creation of new ghettos for certain nationalities, but displacements freely consented to, or rather demanded by certain nationalities or parts of nationalities. The dispersed Jews who would want to be reassembled in the same community will find a sufficiently extensive and rich spot under the sun. The same possibility will be opened for the Arabs, as for all other scattered nations. *National topography will become a part of the planned economy.* This is the grand historical perspective that I envisage. To work for international socialism means also to work for the solution of the Jewish question.

You ask me if the Jewish question still exists in the USSR. Yes, it exists, just as the Ukrainian, the Georgian, even the Russian questions exist there. The omnipotent bureaucracy stifles the development of national culture just as it does the whole of culture. Worse still, the country of the great proletarian revolution is now passing through a period of profound reaction. If the revolutionary wave revived the finest sentiments of human solidarity, the Thermidorian reaction has stirred up all that is low, dark and backward in this agglomeration of 170 million people. To reinforce its domination the bureaucracy does not even hesitate to resort in a scarcely camouflaged manner to chauvinistic tendencies, above all to anti-Semitic ones. The latest Moscow trial, for example, was staged with the hardly concealed design of presenting internationalists as faithless and lawless Jews who are capable of selling themselves to the German Gestapo.

Since 1925 and above all since 1926, anti-Semitic demagogy, well camouflaged, unattackable, goes hand in hand with symbolic trials against avowed pogromists. You ask me if the old Jewish petty bourgeoisie in the USSR has been socially assimilated by the new Soviet environment. I am indeed at a loss to give you a clear reply. The social and national statistics in the USSR are extremely tendentious. They serve not to set forth the truth, but above all to glorify the leaders, the chiefs, the creators of happiness. An important part of the Jewish petty bourgeoisie has been absorbed by the formidable apparatuses of the state, industry, commerce, the cooperatives, etc., above all in their lower and middle layers. This fact engenders an anti-Semitic state of feeling and the leaders manipulate it with a cunning skill in order to canalize and to direct especially against the Jews the existing discontent against the bureaucracy.

On Birobidjan I can give you no more than my personal evaluations. I am not acquainted with this region and still less with the conditions in which the Jews have settled there. In any case it can be no more than a very limited experience. The USSR alone would still be too poor to resolve its own Jewish question, even under a regime much more socialist than the present one. The Jewish question, I repeat, is indissolubly bound up with the complete emancipation of humanity. Everything else that is done in this domain can only be a palliative and often even a two-edged blade, as the example of Palestine shows.

Thermidor and anti-Semitism

This article, written February 22, 1937, appeared in The New International, *May 1941.*

At the time of the last Moscow trial I remarked in one of my statements that Stalin, in the struggle with the Opposition, exploited the anti-Semitic tendencies in the country. On this subject I received a series of letters and questions which were, by and large—there is no reason to hide the truth—very naive. "How can one accuse the Soviet Union of anti-Semitism?" "If the USSR is an anti-Semitic country, is there anything left at all?" That was the dominant note of these letters. These people raise objections and are perplexed because they are accustomed to counterpose fascist anti-Semitism with the emancipation of the Jews accomplished by the October Revolution. To these people it now appears that I am wresting from their hands a magic charm. Such a method of reasoning is typical of those who are accustomed to vulgar, nondialectical thinking. They live in a world of immutable abstractions. They recognize only that which suits them: the Germany of Hitler is the absolutist kingdom of anti-Semitism; the USSR, on the contrary, is the kingdom of national harmony. Vital contradictions, changes, transitions from one condition to another, in a word, the actual historical processes escape their lackadaisical attention.

It has not yet been forgotten, I trust, that anti-Semitism was quite widespread in Czarist Russia among the peasants, the petty bourgeoisie of the city, the intelligentsia and the more backward strata of the working class. "Mother" Russia was renowned not only for her periodic Jewish pogroms but also for the existence of a considerable number of anti-Semitic publications which, in that day, enjoyed a wide circulation. The October Revolution abolished the outlawed status against the Jews. That, however, does not at all mean that with one blow it swept out anti-Semitism. A long and persistent struggle against religion has failed to prevent suppliants even today from crowding thousands and thousands of churches, mosques and synagogues. The same situation prevails in the sphere of national prejudices. Legislation alone does not change people. Their thoughts, emotions, outlook depend upon tradition, material conditions of life, cultural level, etc. The Soviet regime is not yet twenty years old. The older half of the population was educated under Czarism. The younger half has inherited a great deal from the older. These general historical conditions in themselves should make any thinking person realize that, despite the model legislation of the October Revolution, it is impossible that national and chauvinist prejudices, particularly anti-Semitism, should not have persisted strongly among the backward layers of the population.

But this is by no means all. The Soviet regime, in actuality, initiated a series of new phenomena which, because of the poverty and low cultural level of the population, were capable of generating anew, and did in fact generate, anti-Semitic moods. The Jews are a typical city population. They comprise a considerable percentage of the city population in the Ukraine, in White Russia and even in Great Russia. The Soviet, more than any other regime in the world, needs a very great number of civil servants. Civil servants are recruited from the more cultured city population. Naturally the Jews occupied a disproportionately large place among the bureaucracy and particularly so in its lower and middle levels. Of course we can close our eyes to that fact and limit ourselves to vague generalities about the equality and brotherhood of all races. But an ostrich policy will not advance us a single step. *The hatred of the peasants and the workers for the bureaucracy is a fundamental fact in Soviet life.* The despotism of the regime, the persecution of every critic, the stifling of every living thought, finally the judicial frame-ups are merely the reflection of this basic fact. Even by *a priori* reasoning it is impossible not to conclude that the hatred for the bureaucracy would assume an anti-Semitic color, at least in those places where the Jewish functionaries compose a significant percentage of the population and are thrown into relief against the broad background of the peasant masses. In 1923 I proposed to the party conference of the Bolsheviks of the Ukraine that functionaries should be able to speak and write the idiom of the surrounding population. How many ironical remarks were made about this proposal, in the main by the Jewish intelligentsia who spoke and read Russian and did not wish to learn the Ukrainian language! It must be admitted that in that respect the situation has changed considerably for the better. But the national composition of the bureaucracy changed little, and what is immeasurably more important, the antagonism between the population and the bureaucracy has grown monstrously during the past ten to twelve years. All serious and honest observers, especially those who have lived among the toiling masses for a long time, bear witness to the existence of anti-Semitism, not only of the old and hereditary, but also of the new, "Soviet" variety.

The Soviet bureaucrat feels himself morally in a beleaguered camp. He attempts with all his strength to break through from his isolation. The politics of Stalin, at least to the extent of 50 percent, is dictated by this urge. To wit: (1) the pseudosocialist demagogy ("Socialism is already accomplished," "Stalin gave, gives and will give the people a happy life," etc.); (2) political and economic measures designed to build around the bureaucracy a broad layer of a new aristocracy (the disproportionately high wages of the Stakhanovites, military ranks, honorary orders, the new "nobility," etc.); and (3) catering to the national feelings and prejudices of the backward layers of the population.

The Ukrainian bureaucrat, if he himself is an indigenous Ukrainian, will, at the critical moment, inevitably try to emphasize that he is a brother to the *muzhik* and the peasant—not some sort of foreigner and under no circumstances a Jew. Of course there is not—alas!—a grain of "socialism" or even of elementary democracy in such an attitude. But that's precisely the nub of the question. The privileged bureaucracy, fearful of its privileges, and consequently completely demoralized, represents at present *the most antisocialist and most antidemocratic stratum of Soviet society.* In the struggle for its self-preservation it exploits the most ingrained prejudices and the most benighted instincts. If in Moscow, Stalin stages trials which accuse the Trotskyites of plotting to poison the workers, then it is not difficult to imagine to what foul depths the bureaucracy can resort in some Ukrainian or central Asiatic hovel!

He who attentively observes Soviet life, even if only through official publications, will from time to time see bared in various parts of the country hideous bureaucratic abscesses: bribery, corruption, embezzlement, murder of persons whose existence is embarrassing to the bureaucracy, violation of women and the like. Were we to slash vertically through, we would see that every such abscess resulted from the bureaucratic stratum. Sometimes Moscow is constrained to resort to demonstration trials. In all such trials the Jews inevitably comprise a significant percentage, in part because, as was already stated, they make up a great part of the bureaucracy and are branded with its odium, partly because, impelled by the instinct for self-preservation, the leading cadre of the bureaucracy at the center and in the provinces strives to divert the indignation of the working masses from itself to the Jews. This fact was known to every critical observer in the USSR as far back as ten years ago, when the Stalin regime had hardly as yet revealed its basic features.

The struggle against the Opposition was for the ruling clique a question of life and death. The program, principles, ties with the masses, everything was rooted out and cast aside because of the anxiety of the new ruling clique for its self-preservation. These people stop at nothing in order to guard their privileges and power. Recently an announcement was released to the whole world, to the effect that my youngest son, Sergei Sedov, was under indictment for plotting a mass poisoning of the workers. Every normal person will conclude: people capable of preferring such a charge have reached the last degree of moral degradation. Is it possible in that case to doubt even for a moment that these same accusers are capable of fostering the anti-Semitic prejudices of the masses? Precisely in the case of my son, both these depravities are united. It is worthwhile to consider this case. From the day of their birth, my sons bore the name of their mother (Sedov). They never used any other name—neither at elementary school, nor at the university, nor in their later life. As for me, during the past thirty-four years I have borne the name of Trotsky. During the Soviet period no one ever called me by the name of my father (Bronstein), just as no one ever called Stalin Dzhugashvili. In order not to oblige my sons to change their name, I, for "citizenship" requirements, took on the name of my wife (which, according to the Soviet law, is fully permissible). However, after my son, Sergei Sedov, was charged with the utterly incredible accusation of plotting to poison workers, the GPU announced in the Soviet and foreign press that the "real" (!) name of my son is not Sedov but Bronstein.

If these falsifiers wished to emphasize the connection of the accused with me, they would have called him Trotsky since politically the name Bronstein means nothing at all to anyone. But they were out for other game; that is, they wished to emphasize my Jewish origin and the semi-Jewish origin of my son. I paused at this episode because it has a vital and yet not at all exceptional character. The whole struggle against the Opposition is full of such episodes.

Between 1923 and 1926, when Stalin, with Zinoviev and Kamenev, was still a member of the "Troika," the play on the strings of anti-Semitism bore a very cautious and masked character. Especially schooled orators (Stalin already then led an underhanded struggle against his associates) said that the followers of Trotsky are petty bourgeois from "small towns," without defining their race. Actually that was untrue. The percentage of Jewish intellectuals in the Opposition was in no case any greater than that in the party and in the bureaucracy. It is sufficient to name the leaders of the Opposition for the years 1923–25: I.N. Smirnov, Serebryakov, Rakovsky, Piatakov, Preobrazhensky, Krestinsky, Muralov, Beloborodov, Mrachkovsky, V. Yakovlev, Sapronov, V.M. Smirnov, Ishtchenko—fully indigenous Russians. Radek at that time was only half-sympathetic. But, as in the trials of the grafters and other scoundrels, so at the time of the expulsions of the Opposition from the party, the bureaucracy purposely emphasized the names of Jewish members of casual and secondary importance. This was quite openly discussed in the party, and, back in 1925, the Opposition saw in this situation the unmistakable symptom of the decay of the ruling clique.

After Zinoviev and Kamenev joined the Opposition the situation changed radically for the worse. At this point there opened wide a perfect chance to say to the workers that at the head of the Opposition stand three "dissatisfied

Jewish intellectuals." Under the direction of Stalin, Uglanov in Moscow and Kirov in Leningrad carried through this line systematically and almost fully in the open. In order the more sharply to demonstrate to the workers the differences between the "old" course and the "new," the Jews, even when unreservedly devoted to the general line, were removed from responsible party and Soviet posts. Not only in the country but even in Moscow factories the baiting of the Opposition back in 1926 often assumed a thoroughly obvious anti-Semitic character. Many agitators spoke brazenly: "The Jews are rioting." I received hundreds of letters deploring the anti-Semitic methods in the struggle with the Opposition. At one of the sessions of the Politburo I wrote Bukharin a note: "You cannot help knowing that even in Moscow in the struggle against the Opposition, methods of Black Hundred demagogues (anti-Semitism, etc.) are utilized." Bukharin answered me evasively on that same piece of paper: "Individual instances, of course, are possible." I again wrote: "I have in mind not individual instances but a systematic agitation among the party secretaries at large Moscow enterprises. Will you agree to come with me to investigate an example of this at the factory 'Skorokhod' (I know of a number of other such examples)." Bukharin answered, "All right, we can go." In vain I tried to make him carry out the promise. Stalin most categorically forbade him to do so. In the months of preparations for the expulsions of the Opposition from the party, the arrests, the exiles (in the second half of 1927), the anti-Semitic agitation assumed a thoroughly unbridled character. The slogan, "Beat the Opposition," often took on the complexion of the old slogan "Beat the Jews and save Russia." The matter went so far that Stalin was constrained to come out with a printed statement which declared: "We fight against Trotsky, Zinoviev and Kamenev not because they are Jews but because they are

Oppositionists," etc. To every politically thinking person it was completely clear that this consciously equivocal declaration, directed against "excesses" of anti-Semitism, did at the same time with complete premeditation nourish it. "Do not forget that the leaders of the Opposition are—Jews." That was the *meaning* of the statement of Stalin, published in all Soviet journals.

When the Opposition, to meet the repressions, proceeded with a more decisive and open struggle, Stalin, in the form of a very significant "jest," told Piatakov and Preobrazhensky: "You at the least are fighting against the C.E., openly brandishing your axes. That proves *your 'orthodox'* action. [The word used by Stalin in Russian refers to the Greek Orthodox Church.—Tr.] Trotsky works slyly and not with a hatchet." Preobrazhensky and Piatakov related this conversation to me with strong revulsion. Dozens of times Stalin attempted to counterpose the "orthodox" core of the Opposition to me.

The well-known German radical journalist, the former editor of *Aktion,* Franz Pfemfert, at present in exile, wrote me in August, 1936:

"Perhaps you remember that several years ago in *Aktion* I declared that many actions of Stalin can be explained by his anti-Semitic tendencies. The fact that in this monstrous trial he, through *Tass,* managed to 'correct' the names of Zinoviev and Kamenev represents, by itself, a gesture in typical Streicher style. In this manner Stalin gave the 'Go' sign to all anti-Semitic, unscrupulous elements."

In fact the names, Zinoviev and Kamenev, it would seem, are more famous than the names of Radomislyski and Rozenfeld. What other motive could Stalin have had to make known the "real" names of his victims, except to play with anti-Semitic moods? Such an act, and without the slightest legal justification, was, as we have seen, likewise committed over the name of my son. But, undoubtedly, the most astonishing thing is the fact that all four "terrorists" allegedly sent by me from abroad turned out to be Jews and—at the same time—agents of the anti-Semitic Gestapo! Inasmuch as I have never actually seen any of these unfortunates, it is clear that the GPU deliberately selected them because of their racial origin. And the GPU does not function by virtue of its own inspiration!

Again: if such methods are practiced at the very top where the personal responsibility of Stalin is absolutely unquestionable, then it is not hard to imagine what transpires in the ranks, at the factories, and especially at the *kolkhozes*. And how can it be otherwise? The physical extermination of the older generation of the Bolsheviks is, for every person who can think, an incontrovertible expression of Thermidorian reaction, and in its most advanced stage at that. History has never yet seen an example when the reaction following the revolutionary upsurge was not accompanied by the most unbridled chauvinistic passions, anti-Semitism among them.

In the opinion of some "Friends of the USSR," my reference to the exploitation of anti-Semitic tendencies by a considerable part of the present bureaucracy represents a malicious invention for the purpose of a struggle against Stalin. It is difficult to argue with professional "friends" of the bureaucracy. These people deny the existence of a Thermidorian reaction. They accept even the Moscow trials at face value. There are "friends" who visit the USSR with special intention of not seeing the spots on the sun. Not a few of these receive special pay for their readiness to see only what is pointed out to them by the finger of the bureaucracy. But woe to those workers, revolutionists, socialists, democrats who, in the words of Pushkin, prefer "a delusion which exalts us" to the bitter truth. A healthy revolutionary optimism has no need for illusions. One must face life as it is. It is necessary to find in reality itself the force to overcome its reactionary and barbaric features. That is what Marxism teaches us.

Some would-be "pundits" have even accused me of "suddenly" raising the "Jewish question" and of intending to create some kind of ghetto for the Jews. I can only shrug my shoulders in pity. I have lived my whole life outside of Jewish circles. I have always worked in the Russian workers' movement. My native tongue is Russian. Unfortunately, I have not even learned to read Jewish. The Jewish question therefore has never occupied the center of my attention. But that does not mean that I have the right to be blind to the Jewish problem which exists and demands solution. "The Friends of the USSR" are satisfied with the creation of Birobidjan. I will not stop at this point to consider whether it was built on a sound foundation, and what type of regime exists there. (Birobidjan cannot help reflecting all the vices of bureaucratic despotism.) But not a single progressive, thinking individual will object to the USSR designating a special territory for those of its citizens who feel themselves to be Jews, who use the Jewish language in preference to all others and who wish to live as a compact mass. Is this or is this not a ghetto? During the period of Soviet democracy, of completely *voluntary* migrations, there could be no talk about ghettos. But the Jewish question, by the very manner in which settlements of Jews occurred, assumes an international aspect. Are we not correct in saying that a world socialist federation would have to make possible the creation of a "Birobidjan" for those Jews who wish to have their own autonomous republic as the arena for their own culture? It may be presumed that a socialist democracy will not resort to compulsory assimilation. It may very well be that within two or three generations the boundaries of an independent Jewish republic, as of many other national regions, will be erased. I have neither time nor desire to meditate on this. Our descendants will know better than we what to do. I have in mind a transitional historical period when the Jewish question, as such, is still acute and demands adequate measures from a world federation of workers' states. The very same methods of solving the Jewish question which under decaying capitalism have a utopian and reactionary character (Zionism), will, under the regime of a socialist federation, take on a real and salutary meaning. This is what I wanted to point out. How could any Marxist, or even any consistent democrat, object to this?

Appeal to American Jews menaced by fascism and anti-Semitism

This appeal, written December 22, 1938, was printed in the magazine Fourth International, *December 1945.*

Dear Friend:

Father Coughlin, who apparently tries to demonstrate that the absolute idealistic moral does not prevent man from being the greatest rascal, has declared over the radio that in the past I received enormous sums of money for the revolution from the Jewish bourgeoisie in the United States. I have already answered in the press that this is false. I did not receive such money, not, of course, because I would have refused financial support for the revolution, but because the Jewish bourgeoisie did not offer this support. The Jewish bourgeoisie remains true to the principle: *not to give,* even now when its head is concerned. Suffocating in its own contradictions, capitalism directs enraged blows against the Jews; moreover a part of these blows fall upon the Jewish bourgeoisie in spite of all its past "service" for capitalism. Measures of a philanthropical nature for refugees become less and less efficacious in comparison with the gigantic dimension of the evil burdening the Jewish people.

Now it is the turn of France. The victory of fascism in this country would signify a vast strengthening of reaction, and a monstrous growth of violent anti-Semitism in all the world, above all in the United States. The number of countries which expel the Jews grows without cease. The number of countries able to accept them decreases. At the same time the exacerbation of the struggle intensifies. It is possible to imagine without difficulty what awaits the Jews at the mere outbreak of the future world war. But even without war the next development of world reaction signifies with certainty the *physical extermination of the Jews.*

Palestine appears a tragic mirage, Birobidjan a bureaucratic farce. The Kremlin refuses to accept refugees. The "antifascist" congresses of old ladies and young careerists do not have the slightest importance. Now more than ever, the fate of the Jewish people—not only their political but also their physical fate—is indissolubly linked with the emancipating struggle of the international proletariat. Only audacious mobilization of the workers against reaction, creation of workers' militia, direct physical resistance to the fascist gangs, increasing self-confidence, activity and audacity on the part of all the oppressed can provoke a change in the relation of forces, stop the world wave of fascism, and open a new chapter in the history of mankind.

The Fourth International was the first to proclaim the danger of fascism and to indicate the way of salvation. The

Fourth International calls upon the Jewish popular masses not to delude themselves but to face openly the menacing reality. Salvation lies only in revolutionary struggle. The "sinews" of revolutionary struggle, as of war, are funds. With the progressive and perspicacious elements of the Jewish people rests the obligation to come to the help of the revolutionary vanguard. Time presses. A day is now equivalent to a month or even to a year. What thou doest, do quickly!

Imperialism and anti-Semitism

These are excerpts from The Imperialist War and the Proletarian World Revolution, *the Manifesto of the Emergency Conference of the Fourth International, held in May 1940. The Manifesto was published in* Social-ist Appeal, *June 29, 1940; it is also reprinted in* Writings of Leon Trotsky (1939–40), *(Pathfinder, 1969, 1973).*

The world of decaying capitalism is overcrowded. The question of admitting a hundred extra refugees becomes a major problem for such a world power as the United States. In an era of aviation, telegraph, telephone, radio, and television, travel from country to country is paralyzed by passports and visas. The period of the wasting away of foreign trade and the decline of domestic trade is at the same time the period of the monstrous intensification of chauvinism and especially of anti-Semitism. In the epoch of its rise, capitalism took the Jewish people out of the ghetto and utilized them as an instrument in its commercial expansion. Today decaying capitalist society is striving to squeeze the Jewish people from all its pores; seventeen million individuals out of the two billion populating the globe, that is, less than one percent, can no longer find a place on our planet! Amid the vast expanses of land and the marvels of technology, which has also conquered the skies for man as well as the earth, the bourgeoisie has managed to convert our planet into a foul prison. . . .

The struggle for "living room" is nothing but camouflage for imperialist expansion, that is, the policy of annexation and plunder. The racial justification for this expansion is a lie; National Socialism changes its racial sympathies and antipathies in accordance with strategic considerations. A somewhat more stable element in fascist propaganda is, perhaps, anti-Semitism, which Hitler has given a zoological form, discovering the true language of "race" and "blood" in the dog's bark and the pig's grunt. Not for nothing did Frederick Engels label anti-Semitism the "socialism of idiots"! The sole feature of fascism which is not counterfeit is its will to power, subjugation, and plunder. Fascism is a chemically pure distillation of the culture of imperialism. . . .

After five years of the crudest fawning upon the democracies, when the whole of "communism" was reduced to the monotonous indictment of fascist aggressors, the Comintern suddenly discovered in the autumn of 1939 the criminal imperialism of the Western democracies. Left about face! From then on not a single word of condemnation about the destruction of Czechoslovakia and Poland, the seizure of Denmark and Norway and the shocking bestialities inflicted by Hitler's gangs on the Polish and Jewish people! Hitler was made out to be a peace-loving vegetarian continually being provoked by the Western imperialists.

THE FIGHT AGAINST FASCISM

THE STRUGGLE AGAINST FASCISM IN GERMANY
Leon Trotsky

Writing in the heat of struggle against the rising Nazi movement, a central leader of the Russian revolution examines the class roots of fascism and advances a revolutionary strategy to combat it. $32

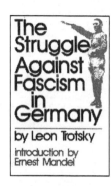

The Struggle Against Fascism in Germany
by Leon Trotsky
introduction by Ernest Mandel

THE SOCIALIST WORKERS PARTY IN WORLD WAR II
WRITINGS AND SPEECHES, 1940–43
James P. Cannon

Preparing the communist movement in the United States to stand against the patriotic wave inside the workers movement supporting the imperialist slaughter and to campaign against wartime censorship, repression, and antiunion assaults. $25

James P. Cannon
WRITINGS AND SPEECHES, 1940–43
The Socialist Workers Party in World War II

THE JEWISH QUESTION
A MARXIST INTERPRETATION
Abram Leon

Traces the historical rationalizations of anti-Semitism to the fact that Jews—in the centuries preceding the domination of industrial capitalism—emerged as a "people-class" of merchants and moneylenders. Leon explains why the propertied rulers incite renewed Jew-hatred today. $22

WHAT IS AMERICAN FASCISM?
James P. Cannon and Joseph Hansen

Analyzing examples from the 20th century—Father Charles Coughlin, Jersey City mayor Frank Hague, and Sen. Joseph McCarthy—this collection looks at the features distinguishing fascist movements and demagogues in the US from the 1930s to today. $8

New International

A MAGAZINE OF MARXIST POLITICS AND THEORY

NEW INTERNATIONAL NO. 12
CAPITALISM'S LONG HOT WINTER HAS BEGUN
Jack Barnes
and "Their Transformation and Ours," Resolution of the Socialist Workers Party

Today's sharpening interimperialist conflicts are fueled both by the opening stages of what will be decades of economic, financial, and social convulsions and class battles, and by the most far-reaching shift in Washington's military policy and organization since the US buildup toward World War II. Class-struggle-minded working people must face this historic turning point for imperialism, and draw satisfaction from being "in their face" as we chart a revolutionary course to confront it. $16. Also in Spanish, French, and Swedish. *Capitalism's Long Hot Winter Has Begun* is available in Arabic.

NEW INTERNATIONAL NO. 13
OUR POLITICS START WITH THE WORLD
Jack Barnes

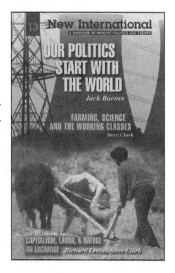

The huge economic and cultural inequalities between imperialist and semicolonial countries, and among classes within almost every country, are produced, reproduced, and accentuated by the workings of capitalism. For vanguard workers to build parties able to lead a successful revolutionary struggle for power in our own countries, says Jack Barnes in the lead article, our activity must be guided by a strategy to close this gap.

Also in No. 13: "Farming, Science, and the Working Classes" *by Steve Clark.* $14. Also in Spanish, French, and Swedish.

From the dictatorship of capital...

The Communist Manifesto

Karl Marx, Frederick Engels

Founding document of the modern revolutionary workers movement, published in 1848. Why communism is not a set of preconceived principles but the line of march of the working class toward power—a line of march "springing from an existing class struggle, a historical movement going on under our very eyes." $5. Also in Spanish, French, and Arabic.

State and Revolution

V.I. Lenin

"The relation of the socialist proletarian revolution to the state is acquiring not only practical political importance," wrote V.I. Lenin in this booklet just months before the October 1917 Russian Revolution. It also addresses the "most urgent problem of the day: explaining to the masses what they will have to do to free themselves from capitalist tyranny." In *Essential Works of Lenin*. $12.95

Their Trotsky and Ours

Jack Barnes

To lead the working class in a successful revolution, a mass proletarian party is needed whose cadres, well beforehand, have absorbed a world communist program, are proletarian in life and work, derive deep satisfaction from doing politics, and have forged a leadership with an acute sense of what to do next. This book is about building such a party. $16. Also in Spanish and French.

www.pathfinderpress.com

...to the dictatorship of the proletariat

Lenin's Final Fight
Speeches and Writings, 1922–23
V.I. Lenin

In 1922 and 1923, V.I. Lenin, central leader of the world's first socialist revolution, waged what was to be his last political battle. At stake was whether that revolution would remain on the proletarian course that had brought workers and peasants to power in October 1917—and laid the foundations for a truly worldwide revolutionary movement of toilers organizing to emulate the Bolsheviks' example. $20. Also in Spanish.

Trade Unions: Their Past, Present, and Future
Karl Marx

Apart from being instruments "required for guerrilla fights between capital and labor," the unions "must now act deliberately as organizing centers of the working class in the broad interest of its complete emancipation," through revolutionary political action. Drafted by Marx for the First International's founding congress in 1866, this resolution appears in *Trade Unions in the Epoch of Imperialist Decay* by Leon Trotsky. $16

The History of the Russian Revolution
Leon Trotsky

The social, economic, and political dynamics of the first socialist revolution as told by one of its central leaders. How, under Lenin's leadership, the Bolshevik Party led the overturn of the monarchist regime of the landlords and capitalists and brought to power a government of the workers and peasants. Unabridged, 3 vols. in one. $38. Also in Russian.

EXPAND *your Revolutionary Library*

The Working Class and the Transformation of Learning
The Fraud of Education Reform under Capitalism
JACK BARNES

"Until society is reorganized so that education is a human activity from the time we are very young until the time we die, there will be no education worthy of working, creating humanity." $3. Also in Spanish, French, Swedish, Icelandic, Farsi, and Greek.

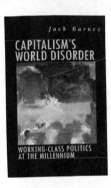

Capitalism's World Disorder
Working-Class Politics at the Millennium
JACK BARNES

Social devastation and financial panic, coarsening of politics, cop brutality, imperialist aggression—all are products not of something gone wrong with capitalism but of its lawful workings. Yet the future can be changed by the united struggle of workers and farmers conscious of their capacity to wage revolutionary battles for state power and transform the world. $25. Also in Spanish and French.

Problems of Women's Liberation
EVELYN REED

Six articles explore the social and economic roots of women's oppression from prehistoric society to modern capitalism and point the road forward to emancipation. $15